FOREWORD

DRAMASCRIPTS are intended for use in secondary schools, amateur theatrical groups and youth clubs, and some will be enjoyed by young people who are still at primary school. They may be used in a variety of ways: read privately for pleasure or aloud in groups; acted in the classroom, church hall or youth club, or in public performances.

ERRAND and THE YOUTH CLUB were among the best plays submitted for a competition run by the Royal Court Theatre in London, in conjunction with *The Young Observer*, and they have been professionally staged in the Theatre Upstairs.

THE YOUTH CLUB, written by Patrick Murray, aged seventeen, deals with a club that is about to be closed down – we see the club, in fact, during the very last hours of its existence. The poignancy of the club's closing moments will affect anyone who has ever been associated in any way with a youth club.

ERRAND, written by Jim Irvin, aged fourteen, started off as an essay for English. 'Then', says Jim, 'I heard of this competition and turned it into a play.' It involves only two people – an old age pensioner, living alone, who is unable to distinguish between his memories and reality; and a delivery boy. It will appeal to all young people, and adults as well, to whom the problems of the senior citizen are as important and as urgent as any we face today.

GUY WILLIAMS
Advisory Editor

CONTENTS

The Youth Club

THE CHARACTERS

BOB, the clubleader, aged about twenty-five
JILL, his wife, aged about twenty-five
BERT HELLY, the caretaker, aged about sixty

TEDDY, aged thirteen
STEVE, aged fourteen
JOHN, aged fifteen
DAVE, aged fifteen
DANNY, aged sixteen   the boys
CHRIS, aged sixteen
PETE, aged sixteen
JIM, aged seventeen
MICK, aged seventeen

TINA, aged twelve
CAROL, aged fourteen
DEBBIE, aged fifteen
JENNY, aged fifteen   the girls
JACKIE, aged fifteen
AMANDA, aged sixteen
FRANNY, aged seventeen

Two ambulance men

THE SET

A school hall with two levels.

On the top level is a counter. Adjacent are the two swing doors which form the main entrance. There are seats and tables around the walls. A record player and a piano are opposite the counter.

There are about four steps down to the lower level. On the lower level there are two table-tennis tables, a dart-board and an exit.

There is nobody in the hall. The ping pong tables are up against a wall in the lower level. The counter is bare.

> *(A key is heard turning in the lock of the swing doors. The bolts slide, and the* **caretaker** *comes in.*
>
> *He glances at the clock; it is six forty-five. He grins, and puts an envelope on the counter. He has a quick look round and goes out.*
>
> *Pause.*
>
> **Bob** *and* **Jill** *come in.* **Bob** *is wearing a tracksuit, and carrying a briefcase. They go behind the counter and* **Bob** *puts his briefcase on it.* **Jill** *is looking fed up.)*

Jill. I don't know why you bother.

Bob. Don't start all that again.

Jill. What's this? *(Picks up the letter)* It's addressed to you. *(Gives it to him)* The caretaker must have left it.

> *(***Bob** *opens it and reads)*

Bob. 'Dear Sir, Mr Bert Helly has made an application concerning the use of our hall for your youth club. He has asked us not to renew your lease for the next term, because of untidiness and vandalism by your members. We have accepted his application so therefore we must inform you that your use of the hall must finish on Friday, 27 March.' But that's today. Tonight's the last night.

Jill. Thank goodness.

Bob. Don't you realise what it means?

Jill. Yes, I do. It means we won't have to spend every Monday, Wednesday and Friday night in this place.

Bob. But what about the kids, what are they going to do?

Jill. I know. They're going to walk about the streets all night, with nowhere to go. They're going to thieve, get up to all sorts of mischief and get into trouble. I know, but what about us? We'll be able to go out for a change. Have a good time together. Look, Bob, I'm sick of this place.

Bob. All right, let's just leave it at that. They'll be here in a minute.

(Pause)

Jill. It's almost seven-thirty.
Bob. Almost.

(Beat)

Jill. When are you going to tell them?
Bob. We'd better wait till it's over. I don't want to spoil their last day.

*(**Jill** kisses him on the cheek)*

Jill. Sorry, Bob.
Bob. I ... Here they come.

*(**Bob** gets a book out of his briefcase. **Teddy** and **Steve** enter.)*

Teddy. Wotcha, Bob, wotcha, Jill.
Bob. Hello.

*(**Teddy** and **Steve** give **Bob** fivepence each. **Bob** marks it down in the book.)*

Bob. Where are the others?
Steve. Inna Wimpey, they won't be long.
Teddy. Come on, Steve, let's put the tables up.
Steve. Yeah, I fancy a game.

(They go down to the lower level.)

Bob *(Smiles)*. They're always the first ones here.
Jill. If they come late they don't get a game of ping pong.

(The other kids come in, all chatting. They start to pay up.)

Jim *(To **Mick**)*. We should have gone dahn the pub.
Mick. I told yer I ain't got enough money.
Jim. You've got two bob, ain't ya?

4

Mick. How can you go into a pub with ten bleeding pence?

Jim. You can get three bags of crisps with that.

Mick. Go ter sleep.

Danny *(To* **Dave***)*. You gonna ask her?

Dave. I dunno.

Danny. Go on, I reckon she's worth it.

Dave. I suppose so.

Danny. Well, bleeding ask her then.

Dave. Just give me time.

Danny. She'll 'ave a beard by the time you ask 'er.

Dave. All right, where is she?

Danny. Right behind yer.

Dave *(In disbelief)*. Yer jokin'.

Danny. 'Ave a look.

*(***Dave** *turns round slowly to see* **Jackie***)*

Dave. Er, hello.

Jackie. Yeah.

Dave. Er, will you go out with me?

Jackie. You must be joking.

(She walks away. **Danny** *starts laughing hilariously.)*

Dave *(To* **Danny***)*. You rat, you knew she was standing there.

Danny *(Still laughing)*. I'm sorry, Dave, I couldn't resist it.

Dave. Just you wait, I'll get you back, don't worry.

Tina *(To* **Carol** *and* **Debbie***)*. You 'eard David Moore's latest?

Carol. No.

Tina. It ain't 'arf good.

Debbie. Wassit called?

Tina. I dunno, my mate told me about it.

Debbie. 'Ow do you know you like it, then?

Tina. 'Course I like it, David Moore's singing it, en he?

Carol. Do me a favour.

Tina. What?

Carol. Try listening to the music for a change. You might notice
  something.

John *(To* **Pete** *and* **Chris***)*. I dare either of you to try and get your arm
  around Amanda.

Chris. No thanks, I'm happy with Debbie.

Pete. Go away. Ask me to get blood out of a stone instead. She is a bigger prude than my Aunt Victoria.

John. I'll do it for a dollar.

Pete. You're on.

Chris. Same here.

(John goes over to Amanda sitting by herself. He sits next to her. She looks away.)

John. Wotcha, Amanda.

Amanda. Hello.

John. Wanna fag?

Amanda. No thanks.

John. Wanna bubble-gum?

Amanda. No thanks.

(Beat)

John. 'Ow about a coke?

Amanda. Okay.

(John goes to the counter and gets a coke)

Chris *(To John)*. It looks good. Wat yer reckon?

Pete. It's not possible.

John *(Giving Amanda her drink)*. Her' yar.

Amanda. Thanks.

John. Mind if I say something?

Amanda. What?

John. I think you're pretty smart.

Amanda. Seriously?

John. Yeah, I really mean it.

Amanda. Thanks.

John. Would you happen to be going out with anyone?

Amanda. No.

John. Well, I was just wondering if I might have a chance?

Amanda. Yes.

John *(Surprised)*. What!

Amanda. Yes, okay.

6

John. I don't beli ... I mean, great!

(He puts his arm around her)

Amanda. Well, aren't you going to give me a kiss?
John. What? Oh, yeah, I er ...

(He kisses her. **Bob** *is looking over, smiling.)*

Bob. We'd better watch them two.
Jill. I think you've got a point there.
Bob. I wish I didn't have to tell them about the letter, Jill, it's going to
    be rotten for me to watch their faces.
Jill. It's not your fault, Bob. They brought it on themselves.
Bob. They smashed two windows playing football in the gym this term.
    We should've replaced them weeks ago.
Jill. It's up to the school to fix them. They took the responsibility for
    damage.
Bob. Well, why did the caretaker want to get rid of us, then?
Jill. He's getting old. He probably doesn't like kids anyway.
Bob. I suppose you're right.
Dave *(To* **Bob***)*. Coke, please.
Bob. Here y'ar, Dave, that's six pence.
Dave. Oh, yeah, can you put it down to next week?

*(***Bob** *turns to* **Jill***, then looks back at* **Dave***)*

Bob. Yes, um—okay, Dave.
Dave. Cheers. By the way, when are we going to get our minibus?
Bob. I'll be telling you about that later.
Dave. When?
Bob. I said later.
Dave. I was only asking.

*(***Dave** *walks away)*

Bob *(To* **Jill***)*. Roll on ten o'clock.

*(***John** *is still sitting next to* **Amanda** *with his arm round her)*

John. Hold on a sec.
Amanda. Where are you going?
John. I've gotta collect some money.

(He gets up and goes to **Chris** *and* **Pete** *who are chatting)*

Right, lads, git your money out.
Chris. 'Ow jer do it?
John. That's a trade secret, ennit?
Chris. I still don't . . .
John. Come on, cough up.

*(***Chris** *gives him the money.* **Pete** *hesitates.)*

Pete. Can I pay yer tomorrow?
John. You always say that, come on.

*(***Pete** *gives him the money reluctantly)*

Pete. Satisfied?
John. Yes sirree.

*(***John** *goes back to* **Amanda***)*

Fancy another coke?

(He grins and rattles the money)

Amanda *(Smiles)*. I wouldn't mind.

*(***Teddy** *and* **Steve** *are playing ping pong in the lower level.* **Jim** *and* **Mick** *are looking on. Beat.)*

Teddy. Hold on, Steve, I wanna go bog.

(He goes out the exit door)

Steve. Hurry up!
Jim *(To* **Mick***)*. We can have a game while he's gone.
Mick. Hang abaht, I've got a better idea. Jus' follow me.

8

(They go through the door. Steve starts playing around with the ping pong ball. Then Mick and Jim come back in, laughing.)

Mick. Did you see that?
Jim. What was it, a half-inch wonder?
Mick. I can just imagine him on top of his bird.
Jim. Yeah, she'd be lying there reading a book.

(Teddy comes in)

Mick. Shush, he's back.
Jim. Oy, Teddy! Come here!
Teddy. What?
Jim. Are you a virgin?
Teddy. Why?
Jim. Come on, jus' tell us.

(Teddy did not know they were watching him)

Teddy. No.

(Jim and Mick burst out laughing again and walk off leaving Teddy dumbfounded)

Franny *(To Jackie)*. I wish Jim would pay a bit more attention to me. He's supposed to be going out with me and he's hardly said a word all night.
Jackie. He's probably gone off you.
Franny. That's nice, you're supposed to be my mate.
Jackie. Well, I didn't mean it like that. What I'm trying to say is you've been going together for too long now.
Franny. What's wrong with that?
Jackie. I don't think he's the serious type.
Franny. Why not?
Jackie. Well, take Joan Norton, for example. Did you see how he flirted with her in the pub that night?
Franny. He said he was drunk.
Jackie. Come off it, you can't get drunk on half o'light.
Franny. Yeah, all right, but that was a month ago.
Jackie. That's what I mean.

9

Franny. I still don't see what difference it makes?
Jackie. Look, Franny, if I were you I'd have a chat with him right now.
Franny. Right then, I won't be long.

(Franny goes over to Jim who is now playing table tennis with Mick)

Franny. Can I talk to you a minute, Jim?
Jim. Inna minute.
Franny. I want to talk to you now.
Jim. I'm trying to have a game of table tennis. Later.
Franny. If you don't speak to me now, it'll be over between us.
Jim. Your service, Mick.
Franny. Did you hear what I said?
Jim. I'm not deaf.

(In a flight of anger Franny catches the ping pong ball and slams her hand down hard on it. The ball gets squashed. Jim grins and puts his hand in his pocket and pulls out another ping pong ball.)

There's plenty more where that came from.

(Franny runs to Jackie, crying)

Mick. That was a bit strong, weren't it?
Jim. I had to get it through to her. She wouldn't take a hint.
Mick. Yeah, but still ...
Jim. Look, never you mind! Just get on with the game.
Mick *(Low)*. Get stuffed!

(Mick walks away and goes over to Franny who is with Jackie)

You all right, Franny?
Jackie. 'Course she's all right. Go away!
Mick. I'm not talking to you.
Jackie. You're all the same.
Mick. Lay orf.

(Mick gets his hanky out; it looks very old and dirty. He offers it to Franny, who is still sobbing. Jackie forces back a laugh.)

10

Mick. Here, Franny.

(Franny looks at it, forces a smile and gives it back)

Franny. Thanks anyway.

(Beat. Jackie moves away.)

Mick. Feeling better now?
Franny. Yeah, I'm all right.
Mick. You like Jim a lot, don't you?
Franny. Yeah.
Mick. How long do you reckon it'd take you to forget about him?

(Franny smiles and looks Mick in the eye)

Franny. With a little bit of help, not very long.

(Mick smiles back. Teddy, Steve, John and Dave are standing, near the exit, chatting. Teddy has a football.)

Teddy *(To Steve, John and Dave)*. Come on, we'll thrash them.
Dave. Come off it.
John. I'm going back to me bird.
Steve. Chicken!
John. All right, then, challenge 'em!
Teddy *(Shouting)*. The little uns challenge the big uns to a game of footer.
Pete *(Who is sitting on a table)*. It's a walkover.
Teddy. No, it's not, it's a challenge.

(Pete gets up and makes his way to the exit followed by Chris, Jim and Danny)

Pete. You asked for it.

(All the boys go out through the exit door except Mick)

Bob *(Shouting after them)*. No shoes in the gym, lads!
Debbie *(To Tina)*. Fancy a game of table tennis?

11

Tina. Nah.

Debbie. 'Ow about darts?

Tina. Nah.

Debbie. I get bored when my Chris has gone.

Tina. Shouldn't have let him go.

Debbie. Can't stop him.

Tina. Why not?

Debbie. He'd probably chuck me.

Tina. Just for keeping him from a game of football?

Debbie. He's always going on about his freedom an' that. 'E says he don't like any prohibitions *(Mispronounced)* or restrictions *(Mispronounced)*.

Tina. Wha's that supposed to mean?

Debbie. Don' arss me.

*(**Bob** notices that **Mick** has not gone up and is still sitting opposite him talking to **Franny**)*

Bob. How about you, Mick? Lost interest in the game?

Mick. Yeah, for the time being.

*(**Bob** smiles then turns to **Jill**)*

Bob. They make us look like puritans the way they carry on.

Jill. I can't remember the last time we were in the back row at the pictures.

Bob. How about tomorrow, then?

Jill *(Laughs)*. It's a date.

*(**Teddy** comes running in)*

Teddy. Bob, git the bandages! John's done his arm in.

*(**John** comes in. He is helped by **Steve**, **Dave** and **Danny**.)*

Bob. Sit down, John. *(**Bob** helps **John** down. He feels the arm.)* Where does it hurt?

John. All over the bleeding place. Argh!

*(**Amanda** comes over; she looks worried)*

12

Amanda. John, are you all right?

John. No. Argh. Leave off, Bob, what're you trying to do?

Bob. Can you roll your sleeve up?

(John does so, slowly. Bob feels it again.)

Bob. I think you've broken it.

John. You can't be far off. All I know is, it's killing me. Ooh!

Bob. Jill, where's the codeine?

(Jill takes a few tablets from the first-aid box and brings them over. Jill makes her way back.)

Ta. Here, John, swallow these.

(John puts them in his mouth, and tries to swallow)

John. I can't, they're stuck in me throat. Where's the water?

Bob. Oh, yes. Jill!

(Jill is already filling a glass)

Jill. Coming!

Bob. Can you phone the hospital as well?

(Jill gives John the water, and he drinks)

Jill. Yes, okay.

Bob *(To John)*. Any better?

John. Not a bit.

Bob. Don't worry, the ambulance will be here soon.

Steve *(Mimicking sirens)*. DAA-DAA-DAA-DAA-DAA. Jus' think, John, it'll be all for you.

John. Lay orf, will ya?

Bob. Steve! *(Bob gets up. To Danny.)* How did it happen?

Danny. He tripped up and hit his arm against the radiator.

Bob. How did he trip up?

Danny. I dunno, maybe he trod on a banana skin or something.

Bob. Come on.

Danny. We was playing footer. Everyone goes over now an' again.

13

Bob. All right then, I'll leave it at that for the time being.
Steve. Can we leave the dock now, your honour?
Bob. Don't be cheeky.

(**Steve** *is talking to* **Danny**)

Steve. When I broke my leg I didn't make half as much noise as 'e did.
Danny. What's wrong with letting it out? It helps get rid of the pain, don' it?
Steve. He don't know what pain is. Have you seen them stitches in me back?
Danny. Don't start that again.
Amanda *(To* **John***)*. How did it happen?
John. I was running down the gym and this radiator jumped on top of me.
Amanda. Come on, John, you can tell me.
John. It doesn't matter. Anyway, I'm glad it happened, in a way.
Amanda. Why?
John. I'll be getting the next six weeks off school.
Amanda. I didn't look at it that way.

(**Bob** *goes back to* **Jill**, *who is behind the counter*)

Bob. What a night!
Jill. It could've been worse.
Bob. It had to happen on the last night. We've been injury-free all term.
Jill. It doesn't matter anyway; it'll be all over at ten o'clock.
Bob. It doesn't seem like it.

(**Jill** *hands* **Bob** *a cigarette and they light up*)

Jill. Bob, I think it might be a good idea to tell the kids now, before John goes. Some of them might be going home a bit earlier than the rest anyway.
Bob. I guess so.

(**Bob** *goes to the middle of the hall, and shouts*)

Can I have everybody sitting down up here. Danny, get the lads from upstairs.

(Everybody comes up to the upper level except **Pete** *and* **Chris,** *who are playing table tennis)*

Bob. That includes you two.
Chris. Let's just finish our game.
Bob. Finish your game later. Come on!

(When everybody is settled and quiet, **Bob** *begins)*

Right, I've got to tell you something which I don't like and I know you won't like it either. I'm just going to be straightforward and tell you that tonight is the last club night.
Dave. Come off it!
Bob. Now shut up, Dave! Just keep quiet for a few minutes, will you? I received a letter earlier on telling me that we can't use the hall any more because of complaints of untidiness and vandalism. I know as well as you do that we have treated this place good and proper.

(Siren can be heard now)

Hold on a minute, lads.

(He goes out. The kids' reactions differ: some are angry; some are sad; some of them are fed up. They talk and argue for about ten seconds and then **Bob** *comes in with two* **ambulance men.** **Amanda** *gives* **John** *a quick kiss before they take him out.)*

John. See yah!

(A few of the kids answer. **Bob** *holds the doors open for the* **ambulance men.** *)*

Bob. Ta ta, John!

(Bob sticks his head out the door and watches the ambulance drive away. Beat.)

Right, listen! Apart from what I've just said, that's it. Sorry, kids, but I can't do nothing about it.

15

Danny. Who complained?
Bob. That's not important.
Danny. 'Course it is. Come on!

(**Bob** *goes into his pocket and pulls out the letter.*)

Bob. Have a look for yourself.

(**Danny** *opens the letter. Beat.*)

Danny. Mr Bert Helly, that's the bleeding caretaker.
Teddy. We ain't done nothing though. He jus' thinks we're vandals an'
  all that. It's all in the ol' bastard's mind. They're all like that.
Bob. Thanks, Teddy, you said it for me. But look, lads, don't take it all
  out on him. He's an old man and as Teddy said, it's probably all in
  his mind, about the vandalism and so on.
Jim. Ain't there nothing we can do?
Jill. Not a thing. Look, kids, it's ten o'clock now so we better . . .
Jim. . . . just go home and forget about it. Right then, see yah, Bob, Jill.

(**Jim** *goes out, the others follow saying goodbye to* **Bob** *and* **Jill**.
When they all go out **Bob** *goes over to* **Jill**.
      Pause.)

Bob. I suppose that's it, then.
Jill. Shall we go?
Bob. Just a minute, I want to leave something for the caretaker.

(*He walks up to the windows and puts his fist through one. He cuts
his hand.* **Jill** *runs up to* **Bob** *and puts her arms round him. Beat.
They pick up the briefcase and go off.*
      *The hall is empty: there is silence for about ten seconds then
the* **caretaker** *comes in. He is grinning. He looks at the clock:
five-past ten. He smiles. He has a quick look around and he sees
the smashed glass. He becomes angry and swears under his breath.
He walks off, locks the doors from the outside and slides the bolts.*)

Errand

THE CHARACTERS

FLANNAGAN, an old man, shabbily dressed
BOY, a delivery boy bringing potatoes

Time. The Present.

Place. Flannagan's room, dirty, cold and dark. Paper is scattered over the floor. On one side a fire, over which there is a mantlepiece where various pots and curios are placed. Next to the fire is a rocking chair with its back to the audience. **Flannagan** is sitting in the chair unseen. On the opposite side of the room there is a door.

(There is a knock at the door. **Flannagan** *does not answer. Long pause. Knock again. Pause. Door opens.* **Boy** *looks in.)*

Boy. Mr Flannagan?
Flannagan. Mmmm?

(He stands up)

Boy. I've brought your order.
Flannagan. Eh?

(He turns and looks at the boy)

Boy. Your order. I'm from Dobson's, the corner shop; this is your
    weekly order.
Flannagan. Eh? No matter. What have you brought?
Boy. Your potatoes.
Flannagan. Potatoes?
Boy. Yes.
Flannagan. I never touch those.
Boy. But they're your order.

*(***Flannagan*** goes across to the* **boy.** *The old man walks crooked and slouched. He stands a few yards away from him. He sticks his head towards him and peers at him. Pause.)*

Flannagan. Potatoes, boy, give you gout, typhoid and brain damage,
    yellow fever or deformed children.

19

(Pause)

Flannagan. Did you know that?
Boy. No, I . . .
Flannagan. . . . Chicken pox, small pox, whooping cough, malaria, cholera and venereal disease. *(Pause)* I had that once you know: too many baked potatoes.
Boy. So why do you order them?
Flannagan. Because I like them.

(Pause)

Where were you last week? You didn't come last week.
Boy. I was ill and another boy had to come.
Flannagan. But he didn't come inside, he left the potatoes outside.
Boy. Well he's new to the job and, besides, I wasn't the only one off sick and he had two rounds to do and didn't have a lot of time.
Flannagan. Time! You always find time to come and talk.
Boy. I only have a few orders to deliver.
Flannagan. He didn't even look round the door and let me know.
Boy. It's a very difficult thing to start a new round. It's only after a few weeks you start to get used to coming round . . . you get confidence.
Flannagan. I was most annoyed about not seeing anyone. I enjoy these little chats. And I didn't get a chance to tell him I didn't want any potatoes that week.
Boy. Didn't you want any?
Flannagan. Yes, I did want some, but that's beside the point. If I did want to cancel the order I couldn't have done. I'd have needed extra if anything last week.
Boy. Why?
Flannagan. I had a few friends over, Mr and Mrs Courtney. Very nice couple. I've known them since we were young. They live in Beechmere Terrace. They came here last week for Sunday dinner. We all sat there and talked about the war.

(He goes over to the table and starts to lay it. He mimes it all. He lays mats and cutlery. He goes to a sideboard and brings in imaginary vegetables and meat. He carries over two invisible plates. He takes a cloth from his arm and carves the unseen joint. He

20

dishes up the vegetables and offers the invisible Courtneys gravy,
sauce and salt. He makes no sound at any time. The whole process
is taken slowly with poise and grace. Finally, **Flannagan** *turns to*
the **boy** *again.)*

A fine meal, an excellent meal. They said they'd never tasted such
food.

(He shakes his head slowly.
Pause.)

I was proud. It took me a long time to prepare. *(Pause)* But they
did not thank me, not a word, not a single word of thanks. That's
bloody gratitude for you! I won't invite them round again. You'd
think they'd say something. Just some courteous remark of
acceptance. Nothing, nothing at all. They just ate the meal, stood
up and left. I tried to get them to talk about the war, but they
wouldn't say anything, they didn't speak. *(He lowers his voice)*
It was heartbreaking. All these years we've been friends. I even
knew Bob Courtney at school. Agnes – his wife – she used to go to
the girl's school next door. He used to say to me 'She's nice, eh
Fred?' He'd often talk about her, but pretend he wasn't at all
bothered with her one way or the other. One day she moved to a
boarding school and he didn't see her for about six years. At first
he was really upset about it, but after a while he seemed to
completely forget about her. Then he started to go out with this
girl he met at a church function. Suddenly they realised who each
other was. They fell in love and married. All that time I've known
them.

(Pause)

And there was no thanks.

(Long pause)

Boy. Well, I'll go now.

(Pause)

Flannagan. Mm? Oh yes! Right then! Wait a minute! Are those potatoes all right? The last lot were full of eyes and they crumbled when you boiled them.

Boy. I don't know. Mr Dobson assures me they are good best-quality potatoes.

Flannagan. Humph! *(He looks in the bag and takes some out)* Look! Here's one covered in eyes. Bah! *(He throws it behind him)* There are a lot here.

Boy. Yes, it's two lots for over Christmas. I won't be coming next week 'cos it's Christmas Day.

Flannagan. Christmas?

(He stands up)

Boy. Yes.

*(***Flannagan** *walks slowly up and down the room)*

Flannagan. Already? My goodness! Last Christmas was an unhappy one. That was during the Blitz.

(The **boy** *shows puzzlement)*

It was when the Courtneys' house was bombed. Both were killed. Sad. I had to get in the Christmas pudding – go round to the corner shop. Maggie and I – you've met my wife – *(He glances towards a pile of clothes by the rocking chair)* we were going to my mother's. There was a family gathering. All of us kids and our wives were getting together, and all our relations – you know the sort of thing. Anyway, I was going down our street when I saw Mr Parslow, a blind man that lived in Beechmere Terrace. He was running. Often I would see him walking down our street, very slowly usually. He'd bang his stick along the walls and fences. He'd negotiate the little children and dogs. He seemed to have difficulty, but every time I saw him he'd cross at exactly the same point, just opposite number 61. When crossing the road, he would hold his stick in the air and walk very slowly across. He'd walk to the end of the road and turn the corner. I've no idea what he did or where he went every day, but five minutes later he'd come back. It was the same in the evenings too. I'd lie in bed and hear his stick clacking on all

22

the fences as he edged his way down the street.

But that day he was running. Running. Shouting. His blank face stared through me as he ran. His arms were outstretched, feeling as he ran. They felt only air. I could see he was going to run into a tree. I ran too. I ran to stop him. As I ran the money flew from my pockets. The coppers and florins spun on the pavement and into the road. The old man held up his stick. It was scratched and the white paint was peeling and blistered. He dropped it and it rolled across the ground and down a drain. He kept whining and moaning. I was reaching out to catch him. I stretched out to grab him, but he came to the edge of the road and tripped. He spun and moaned. One foot went into the road. His ankle twisted and cracked. He collapsed in the gutter. His chest was heaving. The pulsing of his body slowed down and stopped suddenly. He was dead. I knelt down beside him. I stared up and looked to the end of the road. Above the rooftops I could see smoke. In the fading light I could see a difference in the outline of the buildings. Every morning on my way to work I would see Mr Parslow and look up and see the chimneys with the birds sitting on them and singing. Now there were no chimneys. The smoke was thick. I went and stood at the end of Beechmere Terrace. Five houses in a row were bombed and burnt out. Nobody had noticed a bomb so close. Why? There were so many falling, one more bomb was no different. Perhaps people didn't want to hear it. Perhaps they shut their minds at Christmas. Seven people were killed that day. For all I know the houses could have been burning for hours. I went back to our road and picked up the coins. I bought the pudding and walked home. As I came down our street I noticed Mr Parslow had gone. Later on he was found buried in the rubble of his house. It was said he was killed by the roof coming in on him. That was last Christmas.

(Long pause)

Boy. I'd better go, then.
Flannagan. I'll give you the money. Turn your back, boy, you can't be too sure. I don't want you to see where my money is kept.

(He goes over to the mantlepiece. In the centre there is an old radio. He lifts this up and gets out a pile of envelopes and papers.

He sorts through them all but can't find anything. He mutters to himself.)

Where has it gone? It was behind the wireless the other week.

(He gets down on his hands and knees and looks in the coal scuttle and fire place.)

No.

(He goes through some papers on the floor. He lifts up a pile of clothes by the chair.)

Shift yourself, Maggie.

(He picks up some of the papers from the floor and puts them behind the radio. As he does this he knocks a pot off the mantlepiece. It rolls across the floor spilling its contents of coins, buttons, pencils, etc. The **boy** *goes to turn round.)*

No, wait a minute.

*(***Flannagan** *gets down on his knees again and picks up the coins, putting them in the pot)*

Boy. Are you sure you don't want any help?
Flannagan. Quite all right, thank you. Ah, there's one. That's the lot.

(He puts some coins into his hand and replaces the pot on the mantlepiece)

You can turn round now.

*(***Flannagan** *stands. The* **boy** *turns.)*

Here you are.

*(***Flannagan** *gives him the money)*

All right?

Boy. Yeh . . . Wait a minute, this is a threepenny bit.
Flannagan. Of course it is.
Boy. But we don't use these nowadays.
Flannagan. What do you mean, don't use them? That's British money, King's currency.
Boy. No. We use decimal currency, a foreign system.
Flannagan. Foreign? We don't use British money?
Boy. Yes, we do use British money. But coins are called different things.
Flannagan. And there are no threepenny bits?
Boy. Those and pennies were wiped out. Like the halfpenny, half-crown and farthing.
Flannagan. What?
Boy. Don't you remember?
Flannagan. No.
Boy. Well, we have . . . a shilling is five pence, a florin is ten. I can't use this threepenny bit. Got any pennies?
Flannagan. These?
Boy. No, new pennies. There, look, two of these five pence pieces will do.
Flannagan. These bob bits?
Boy. Mm!
Flannagan. Two.
Boy. Yes.
Flannagan. And no change?
Boy. No.

(Pause)

Well, thank you Mr Flannagan. I must go, I have other orders to deliver. See you after Christmas.

(There is no answer.
    Flannagan *goes back to the rocking chair and sits down.)*

Boy. Merry Christmas

(The **boy** *leaves. The chair rocks.* **Flannagan's** *hand rests on the arm of the chair. The rocking of the chair slows down.*
    Flannagan's *hand goes limp and a coin falls to the floor.*
    The chair stops rocking. Long pause.)

25